DEEP SEA FISHING

BY ELLEN FRAZEL

BELLWETHER MEDIA • MINNEAPOLIS, MN

Jump into the cockpit and take flight with Pilot books. Your journey will take you on high-energy adventures as you learn about all that is wild, weird, fascinating, and fun!

This edition first published in 2013 by Bellwether Media, Inc.

No part of this publication may be reproduced in whole or in part without written permission of the publisher. For information regarding permission, write to Bellwether Media, Inc., Attention: Permissions Department, 5357 Penn Avenue South, Minneapolis, MN 55419.

Library of Congress Cataloging-in-Publication Data

Frazel, Ellen.
 Deep sea fishing / by Ellen Frazel.
   p. cm. – (Pilot: outdoor adventures)
 Includes bibliographical references and index.
 Summary: "Engaging images accompany information about deep sea fishing. The combination of high-interest subject matter and narrative text is intended for students in grades 3 through 7"– Provided by publisher.
 ISBN 978-1-60014-890-3 (hardcover : alk. paper)
 1. Big game fishing–Juvenile literature. I. Title.
 SH457.5.F73 2013
 799.16–dc23

                              2012036095

Printed in the United States of America, North Mankato, MN.

TABLE OF CONTENTS

A Prize Catch.......................... 4

Deep Sea Boats
    and Equipment 8

Methods and Rules............... 14

Deep Sea Fishing on
    Dauphin Island................... 20

Glossary 22

To Learn More 23

Index 24

A PRIZE CATCH

Off the coast of the Florida Keys, a deep sea **angler** waits for a bite. A driver steers the boat as the angler watches his line **trolling** in the saltwater behind them. He is hoping for a broadbill swordfish. This great trophy fish can weigh up to 1,000 pounds (450 kilograms)!

Suddenly, the angler feels a powerful tug on the line. He secures his feet in the **fighting chair**. Then he reels the line in with all his strength. His catch puts up a good fight. Eventually, the angler gets the thrashing fish in the boat. It is a prize swordfish!

Wiggle Room

Swordfish are known to fight hard and swim away when hooked. A swordfish angler uses a reel with more than 1 mile (1.6 kilometers) of heavy line!

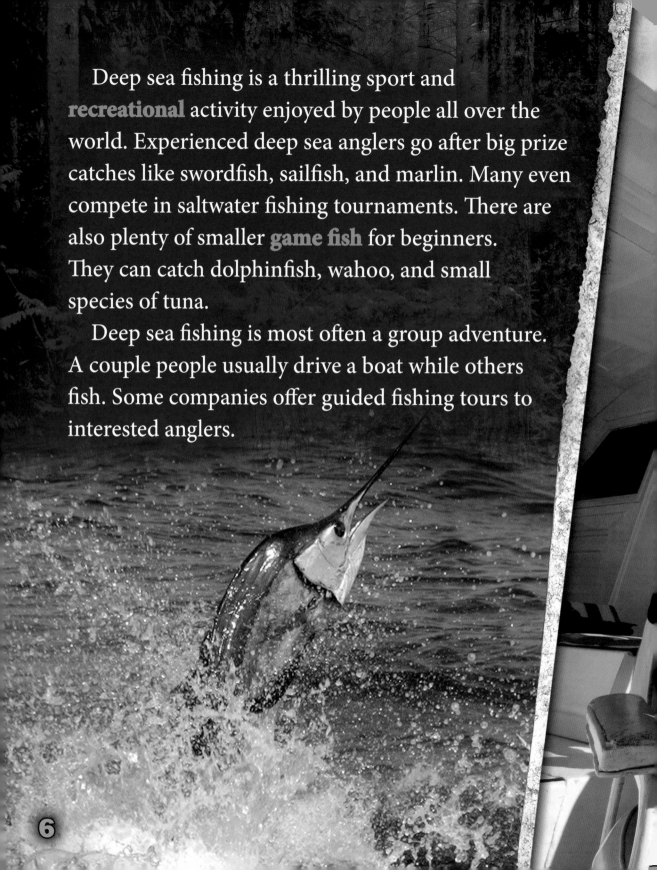

Deep sea fishing is a thrilling sport and **recreational** activity enjoyed by people all over the world. Experienced deep sea anglers go after big prize catches like swordfish, sailfish, and marlin. Many even compete in saltwater fishing tournaments. There are also plenty of smaller **game fish** for beginners. They can catch dolphinfish, wahoo, and small species of tuna.

Deep sea fishing is most often a group adventure. A couple people usually drive a boat while others fish. Some companies offer guided fishing tours to interested anglers.

DEEP SEA BOATS AND EQUIPMENT

Deep sea fishing requires a good boat. Some anglers use boats around 20 feet (6 meters) long. Others prefer larger boats with more powerful motors. These are called sportfishing boats. Some have lengths of 100 feet (30 meters)! Not all anglers own a boat. They can rent boats that come with deep sea fishing equipment and professional captains.

First Deep Sea Fisherman

A marine biologist named Charles Frederick Holder is considered the inventor of deep sea fishing. He caught his first bluefin tuna off the coast of California in 1898.

sportfishing boat

tuna tower

flybridge

fighting chairs

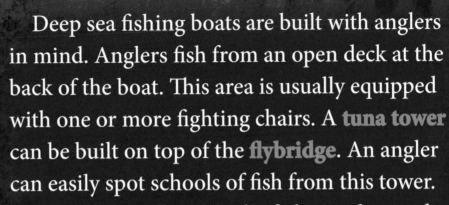

Deep sea fishing boats are built with anglers in mind. Anglers fish from an open deck at the back of the boat. This area is usually equipped with one or more fighting chairs. A **tuna tower** can be built on top of the **flybridge**. An angler can easily spot schools of fish from this tower.

Anglers usually sit in the fighting chairs when fishing. However, some prefer standing with the help of a **harness**. When hauling in a big fish, many people open the **transom door** on the side of their boat.

harness

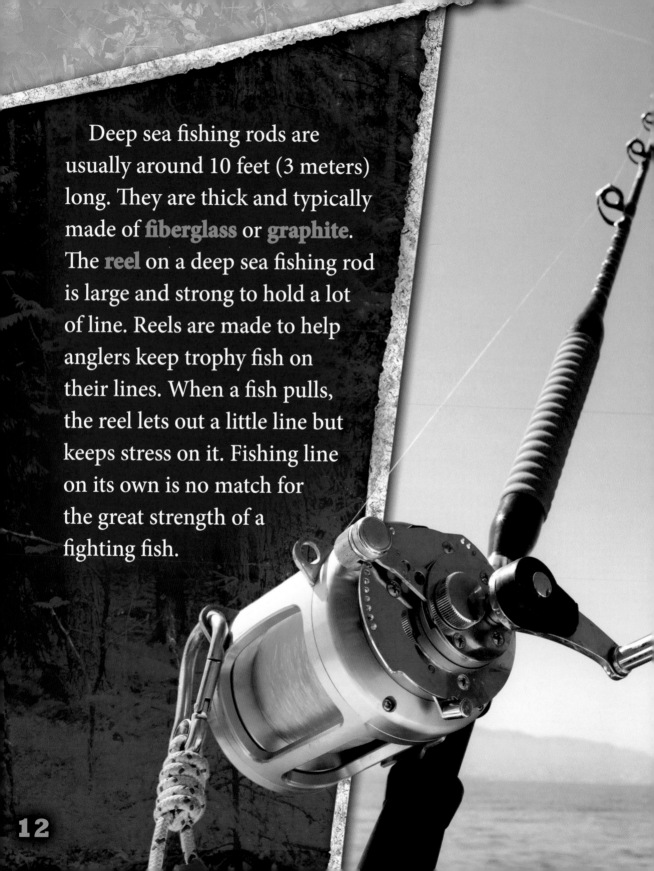

Deep sea fishing rods are usually around 10 feet (3 meters) long. They are thick and typically made of **fiberglass** or **graphite**. The **reel** on a deep sea fishing rod is large and strong to hold a lot of line. Reels are made to help anglers keep trophy fish on their lines. When a fish pulls, the reel lets out a little line but keeps stress on it. Fishing line on its own is no match for the great strength of a fighting fish.

Toughing It Out

Atlantic bluefin tuna are famous for their fight. They are known to battle for several hours before anglers can reel them in!

Atlantic bluefin tuna

METHODS AND RULES

There are different methods used to attract game fish in the deep sea. The most common method is trolling. This involves moving a **lure** or a baited line through the water. Most anglers use **outriggers** to troll lines behind the boat. Other anglers prefer a method called **chumming**. They throw pieces of **baitfish** out into the water to attract a crowd of larger fish. Squids and other live fish are common deep sea bait.

lure

The hard work begins once a fish has been hooked.
The angler reels in the line while the driver steers to
keep the fish behind the boat. Other anglers on the
boat quickly reel in their lines. This is to make sure
these lines do not get tangled with the incoming line.
Once the fish is at the surface, the crew must get it into
the boat. The size of the fish determines if they use their
bare hands, a net, or a **gaff**.

Deep sea anglers need to follow the fishing rules of the state or country where they fish. Many places require anglers to buy licenses and register their boats. **Daily limits** often exist to prevent overfishing. The fishing of threatened species is often banned.

One at a Time

Florida is one state that has strict daily limits. Species like swordfish and billfish are limited to one per person per day.

Safety is also important when deep sea fishing. Responsible anglers check the weather so they don't get caught in a storm. They also know how deep the water is and what the currents are like. Anglers should keep a safe distance from other fishing boats. Everyone on a boat should wear a life jacket.

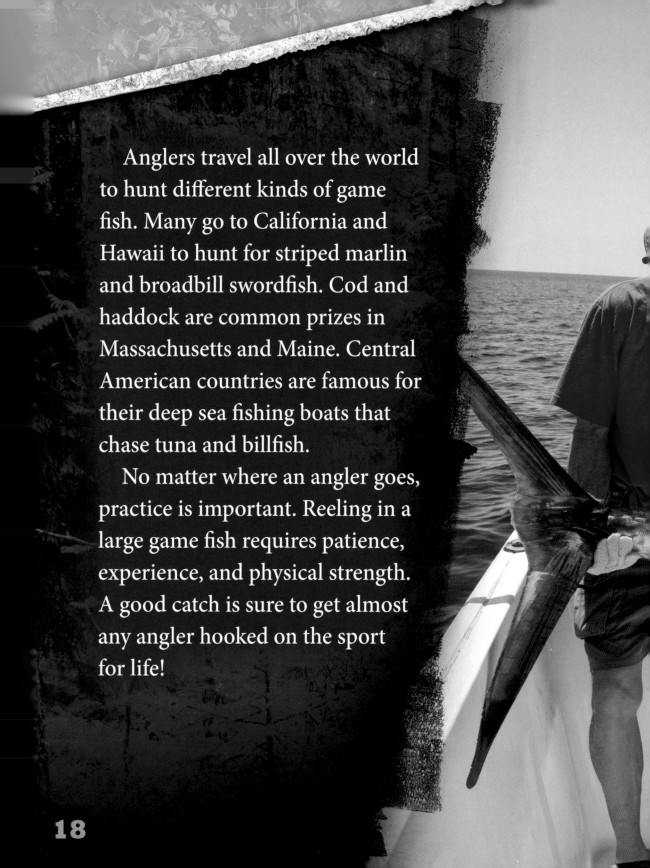

Anglers travel all over the world to hunt different kinds of game fish. Many go to California and Hawaii to hunt for striped marlin and broadbill swordfish. Cod and haddock are common prizes in Massachusetts and Maine. Central American countries are famous for their deep sea fishing boats that chase tuna and billfish.

No matter where an angler goes, practice is important. Reeling in a large game fish requires patience, experience, and physical strength. A good catch is sure to get almost any angler hooked on the sport for life!

DEEP SEA FISHING ON DAUPHIN ISLAND

Dauphin Island off the coast of Alabama is a popular deep sea fishing destination. Anglers come here for the Alabama Deep Sea Fishing Rodeo. This is the world's largest multi-species saltwater fishing tournament. More than 3,000 anglers and 75,000 fans attend the three-day event. The anglers all compete for the Master Angler title. There is also a one-day event for young anglers. Participants 15 years old and younger **cast** their lines in this tournament. The Alabama Deep Sea Fishing Rodeo is a great way for families to experience the excitement of the hunt together.

Alabama

Dauphin Island

N
W E
S

Weighing In

Besides the Master Angler title, there are 30 categories in which anglers can win prizes. First, second, and third places are awarded in each category depending on the weight of the fish.

GLOSSARY

angler—a person who fishes with a hook, line, and reel

baitfish—small fish that attract game fish

cast—to throw fishing line out into a body of water

chumming—a method of fishing that involves throwing bits of chopped up fish into the water to attract other fish to the surface

daily limits—rules that limit an angler to only a certain number of a species of fish per day

fiberglass—a strong material made from a mixture of plastic and glass

fighting chair—a special chair that allows a deep sea angler to have a strong grip on the rod and reel; a fighting chair has a footrest that helps the angler stay steady while using his or her whole body to pull in a fish.

flybridge—a deck above the cabin with navigational equipment

gaff—a pole with a sharp hook used to stab a fish and bring it onto a boat

game fish—fish caught for sport and recreation

graphite—a strong material made from carbon fibers

harness—a piece of safety gear with straps that some anglers wear to stay steady; rods attach to harnesses.

lure—an object that is meant to look like live bait or prey

outriggers—poles that extend out from a boat; outriggers are used to cast multiple lines and enlarge the fishing area.

recreational—done for enjoyment

reel—the part of a fishing rod that controls the line; anglers turn the reel to let the line in or out.

transom door—a door cut into the side of a boat; the transom door can be opened to help bring in a catch.

trolling—a method of fishing that involves moving lines through the water; many deep sea anglers will let their line troll behind the moving boat until they get a bite.

tuna tower—a tower built on top of a flybridge for viewing the surrounding water

TO LEARN MORE

At the Library

Carpenter, Tom. *Saltwater Fishing: Snapper, Mackerel, Bluefish, Tuna, and More*. Minneapolis, Minn.: Lerner, 2013.

Schwartz, Tina P. *Deep-Sea Fishing*. New York, N.Y.: PowerKids Press, 2012.

Thomas, William. *Deep Sea Fishing*. New York, N.Y.: Marshall Cavendish Benchmark, 2010.

On the Web

Learning more about deep sea fishing is as easy as 1, 2, 3.

1. Go to www.factsurfer.com.

2. Enter "deep sea fishing" into the search box.

3. Click the "Surf" button and you will see a list of related Web sites.

With factsurfer.com, finding more information is just a click away.

INDEX

Alabama Deep Sea Fishing
   Rodeo, 20, 21
baitfish, 14
billfish, 16, 18
California, 9, 18
Central America, 18
chumming, 14
cod, 18
daily limits, 16
Dauphin Island, 20
dolphinfish, 6
fight, 4, 5, 12, 13
fighting chair, 4, 10, 11
fishing line, 4, 5, 12, 14,
   15, 20
fishing tours, 6
Florida, 4, 16
flybridge, 10, 11
gaff, 15
game fish, 6, 14, 18
haddock, 18
harness, 11
Hawaii, 18

Holder, Charles Frederick, 9
licenses, 16
lure, 14
Maine, 18
marlin, 6, 18
Massachusetts, 18
outriggers, 14
overfishing, 16
reel, 5, 12
rods, 12
rules, 16
safety, 17
sailfish, 6
sportfishing boats, 8, 9
swordfish, 4, 5, 6, 16, 18
tournaments, 6, 20, 21
transom door, 11
trolling, 4, 14
tuna, 6, 9, 13, 18
tuna tower, 10, 11
wahoo, 6
weather, 17

The images in this book are reproduced through the courtesy of: David Fleetham/Alamy, front cover, p. 14; Miami Herald/MCT/Newscom, p. 5; Juan Martinez, p. 6; Michael DeFreitas Central America/ Alamy, p. 7; Robert Pernell, pp. 8-9; Pacific Stock – Design Pics/Superstock, p. 10; AleksKey, p. 11; holbox, pp. 12-13, 21 (left); DEA Picture Library/Getty Images, p. 13; Ronald C. Modra/ Getty Images, p. 15; 24BY36/Alamy, p. 16; Jefras, p. 17; Carver Mostardi/Agefotostock, pp. 18-19; Seth Resnick/Science Faction/Superstock, p. 21 (right).